CONTENTS

EXPOSED

Exposed

**DEMETRI
WELSH**

To everyone who has ever questioned the world around them, who felt that something wasn't quite right but couldn't put their finger on it.

To the seekers of truth who aren't afraid to dig deeper, challenge the status quo, and face uncomfortable realities.

And to those who have been silenced, ridiculed, or marginalized for daring to ask the hard questions—this book is for you.

May it empower you to keep pushing against the boundaries, to never stop seeking the truth, and to reclaim the power that is rightfully yours.

INTRODUCTION: THE REAL TRUTH

Welcome to the other side of the looking glass, where the stories you've been fed start to unravel and the truth begins to surface. This book isn't for the faint of heart, and it sure as hell isn't for those who are comfortable in their ignorance. What you're holding in your hands is a key—a key that will unlock doors you might have preferred to keep closed, but once opened, there's no going back.

We live in a world where the powerful few have mastered the art of illusion, convincing the masses that they have freedom and control while pulling the strings from the shadows. We're told that history is a straight line, that the world operates in a predictable, logical manner. But deep down, we know that's bullshit. There's a game being played—one that most people don't even know exists. And in this game, the stakes are nothing less than the fate of humanity itself.

In this book, we're going to rip the mask off the carefully constructed facade of global power. We'll dive into the real history behind the secret societies that have shaped world events, exposing the true motives of those who pull the strings. We'll delve into the dark rituals and practices that the elite use to maintain their grip on power, and we'll break down the psychological operations that keep the public docile and distracted. We'll also explore the lost and hidden histories that could completely change how we see ourselves and our place in the universe.

But this isn't just about revealing the ugly truth; it's about reclaiming your power. The system we're going to dissect thrives on ignorance and compliance. It depends on you not questioning the narrative, not challenging the so-called "truths" you've been taught. Once you start seeing the cracks in the story, once you start asking the hard questions, the entire structure begins to shake.

This book is for those who are ready to break free from the illusions that have been spun around them. It's for those who are ready to face the uncomfortable truths that come with real freedom. It's for those who are tired of being played.

So, here we are at the beginning of a journey that will take you places you never expected. A journey that will challenge everything you think you know about the world, about power, and about yourself. But remember, once you start down this path, there's no turning back.

Are you ready to see how deep the rabbit hole goes? Then let's begin.

| 1 |

Chapter 1: The Puppet Masters

Let's get one thing straight right from the start: the world isn't what it seems. The reality you've been presented with, the one that's comfortably wrapped in a blanket of carefully constructed narratives, is a façade. We've all been conditioned to believe that we live in a world where governments run things, where elected officials represent our interests, and where our votes actually matter. But if you pull back the curtain, if you dig a little deeper, you'll find that the real power lies elsewhere.

This chapter is going to take you on a journey through history, pulling together threads that reveal a hidden network of influence that operates far above the visible power structures. We're talking about secret societies, shadowy organizations, and powerful individuals who have been steering the course of human events for centuries, often without anyone outside their circles being the wiser. These are the Puppet Masters—the ones who really run the world.

The Origins of Control

To understand how this hidden network came to be, we need to take a trip back in time. This isn't just about looking at a few decades of history; we're going to go back centuries, even millennia, to trace the origins of control and manipulation.

One of the earliest examples of a secretive group influencing global events can be found in the ancient mystery schools of Egypt, Greece, and Rome. These schools were more than just places of learning; they were centers of power, where the elite gathered to learn esoteric knowledge that was kept from the masses. The priests and scholars who ran these schools were among the first to understand that knowledge is power. They knew that by controlling what people knew—and didn't know—they could shape society to their liking.

These mystery schools laid the groundwork for what would become the template for secret societies throughout history. They understood the power of symbols, rituals, and hidden knowledge, and they used these tools to control the narrative and maintain their influence over rulers and empires. This knowledge was passed down through generations, eventually giving rise to groups that still wield incredible power today.

The Rise of the Illuminati

No discussion of secret societies would be complete without addressing the most infamous of them all: the Illuminati. Founded in 1776 in Bavaria by Adam Weishaupt, the Illuminati was originally conceived as a group dedicated to enlightenment principles, reason, and the pursuit of knowledge. However, it didn't take long for the group to evolve into something far more sinister.

Weishaupt's vision for the Illuminati was to create a new world order, one in which the old institutions of power—monarchies, the church, and even governments—would be dismantled and replaced with a system controlled by a select group of enlightened individuals. The goal was to infiltrate and influence every major institution in society, from the press to the education system, ensuring that the masses were kept in the dark while the Illuminati pulled the strings from behind the scenes.

The Illuminati was officially disbanded in 1785, but its influence didn't disappear. In fact, many believe that the group simply went underground, continuing its work in secret. Over the centuries, the Illuminati has been linked to countless major events, from revolutions to wars, with claims that its members were the ones truly in control. Whether or not the Illuminati as an organization still exists today is up for debate, but the ideas and strategies that Weishaupt pioneered have undoubtedly been adopted by other groups who share the same goals.

The Freemasons and Their Influence

Another key player in the world of secret societies is the Freemasons. With roots dating back to the stonemason guilds of the Middle Ages, the Freemasons have grown into one of the most widespread and influential secret societies in the world. On the surface, the Freemasons present themselves as a fraternal organization dedicated to charity, moral development, and the betterment of society. But behind the closed doors of their lodges, there's a much more complex and secretive world.

Freemasonry is built around a system of degrees, with members ascending through levels of knowledge and influence as they progress. At the higher levels, members are said to gain access to esoteric knowledge and rituals that date back to ancient times. These rituals and symbols, such as the all-seeing eye and the square and compass, are often associated with the occult and have been the subject of endless speculation.

The real power of the Freemasons lies in their ability to network and influence key individuals in positions of authority. Throughout history, Freemasons have counted kings, presidents, and prime ministers among their ranks. The organization's reach extends into politics, finance, and even religion, allowing it to quietly steer the course of history in ways that benefit its members.

One of the most compelling examples of Masonic influence can be found in the founding of the United States. Many of the Founding Fathers, including George Washington and Benjamin Franklin, were

Freemasons, and Masonic symbols are woven into the very fabric of the nation's capital. The layout of Washington, D.C., the design of the Great Seal, and even the dollar bill are all infused with Masonic imagery, leading some to believe that the United States was intended from the start to be a Masonic project—a New Atlantis, where the ideals of the Enlightenment could be realized on a grand scale.

The Bilderberg Group: Modern-Day Kingmakers

While the Illuminati and Freemasons are often relegated to the realm of conspiracy theories, there's another group that operates in the open, yet is shrouded in secrecy: the Bilderberg Group. Founded in 1954, the Bilderberg Group is an annual meeting of some of the most powerful and influential people in the world. Attendees include heads of state, top executives from major corporations, and influential figures in the media, academia, and finance.

The purpose of the Bilderberg meetings is officially described as fostering dialogue between Europe and North America. However, the lack of transparency around what's discussed at these meetings has led to widespread speculation about the group's true agenda. With no press allowed, no official statements released, and participants sworn to secrecy, it's easy to see why the Bilderberg Group has become a focal point for those who believe that a global elite is pulling the strings behind the scenes.

Over the years, many significant political and economic decisions have been linked to Bilderberg meetings. Some claim that elections have been decided, wars have been planned, and economic policies have been shaped within the confines of these secret gatherings. Whether or not the Bilderberg Group is the driving force behind these events, it's clear that the people who attend these meetings have the power to influence the world in profound ways.

The Trilateral Commission and the Council on Foreign Relations

If the Bilderberg Group is the exclusive club of the global elite, then the Trilateral Commission and the Council on Foreign Relations (CFR) are the think tanks that provide the intellectual framework for their actions. Both of these organizations are composed of powerful individuals from politics, business, and academia, and both play a significant role in shaping global policy.

The Trilateral Commission was founded in 1973 by David Rockefeller, Zbigniew Brzezinski, and other influential figures to foster cooperation between North America, Europe, and Japan. The goal was to create a more stable and integrated global order, one in which the interests of these three regions would be aligned. However, critics argue that the real purpose of the Trilateral Commission is to consolidate power among a small group of elites and to undermine national sovereignty in favor of a global government.

The Council on Foreign Relations, founded in 1921, has a similar mission. It serves as a forum for discussing and developing U.S. foreign policy, but its influence extends far beyond the United States. Many of the most powerful and influential figures in global politics, business, and media are members of the CFR, and its recommendations often become policy. The CFR has been accused of promoting a globalist agenda that prioritizes the interests of a global elite over those of individual nations.

Together, the Trilateral Commission and the CFR represent the intellectual and policy-making arm of the global elite. They provide the strategies and frameworks that the Bilderberg Group and other organizations use to implement their vision for the world.

The Power of the Media: Controlling the Narrative

No discussion of global control would be complete without addressing the role of the media. The media is often referred to as the fourth estate—a pillar of democracy that provides a check on power by informing the public and holding leaders accountable. But what happens when the media itself is controlled by those in power?

Over the past century, a handful of corporations have come to dominate the global media landscape. These corporations own newspapers, television networks, radio stations, and online platforms, giving them unprecedented control over what information is disseminated to the public. The consolidation of media ownership has created a situation where a small group of powerful individuals and corporations can shape the narrative, influence public opinion, and suppress dissenting voices.

This control extends beyond traditional media to the digital realm. Social media platforms, search engines, and online news outlets are all subject to the same forces of consolidation and control. Algorithms determine what content is seen and what is buried, creating echo chambers where only certain viewpoints are reinforced. This digital manipulation is a powerful tool for those who wish to control the narrative and keep the public in the dark.

The media doesn't just report the news; it creates reality. By controlling the flow of information, the media can shape how people perceive events, issues, and even themselves. This control is crucial for maintaining the status quo and ensuring that the public remains compliant and unaware of the true nature of power.

The Intersection of Power: Where They All Connect

As we've seen, the world is controlled by a complex web of secret societies, elite organizations, and powerful individuals who operate behind the scenes. But these groups don't exist in isolation; they're interconnected, overlapping, and often working toward the same goals. Members of the Freemasons might attend Bilderberg meetings; CFR members might also be involved in the Trilateral Commission; media moguls might be part of secret societies. This interconnectedness allows for a seamless flow of influence and control, ensuring that the real power remains concentrated in the hands of a few.

These connections aren't always formal or explicit. Often, they're based on shared beliefs, common goals, or mutual interests. The people who belong to these groups understand that their power is magnified when they work together, and they're willing to collaborate, even if it means bending the rules or operating outside the law.

The real power lies not in the institutions themselves, but in the people who run them. It's these individuals, with their networks of influence and their ability to manipulate the system, who are the true Puppet Masters. They understand that by controlling key institutions—be it governments, corporations, or the media—they can control the world.

The Bigger Picture: What This Means for Us

So, what does all of this mean for the average person? If there's a hidden network of powerful individuals and organizations controlling the world, what can we do about it?

First and foremost, it means recognizing that the narrative we've been sold is a lie. The idea that we live in a fair and just world, where the people have power and democracy is the highest ideal, is a comforting illusion. The reality is far more complex and far more unsettling.

But recognizing this truth is the first step toward reclaiming our power. Once we understand that the world is controlled by a hidden network of Puppet Masters, we can start to see through their tactics and resist their influence. We can demand transparency and accountability from our leaders, support independent media that isn't beholden to corporate interests, and educate ourselves about the true nature of power.

Most importantly, we can refuse to be manipulated. By questioning everything, challenging the official narratives, and seeking out the truth for ourselves, we can break free from the illusion and take back control of our lives.

This journey isn't easy, and it's not for everyone. But for those who are willing to face the uncomfortable truths, it's a journey that can lead to real empowerment and freedom. The choice is yours: stay in the dark, or take the first step toward seeing the world as it really is.

Are you ready to see the world through new eyes? Then let's continue this journey, and uncover the truth together.

| 2 |

Chapter 2: Dark Practices of the Elite

Alright, buckle up, because now we're stepping into even darker territory. You might think that secret societies and backdoor political deals are where the rabbit hole ends, but that's just the surface. Beneath the veneer of respectability and power lies a twisted world of rituals, symbols, and practices that most people wouldn't believe unless they saw it with their own eyes. We're talking about the occult, dark rituals, and the disturbing lengths to which the elite will go to maintain their grip on power.

This isn't some Hollywood horror flick—this is real life, and the more you look, the more you realize how deep the connections between power and the occult truly go. From ancient rites to modern-day gatherings in secluded locations, the use of rituals and symbols is a thread that weaves through the very fabric of elite society. It's about power, control, and the manipulation of reality itself. This chapter will uncover the dark underbelly of these practices and expose the shocking truths they don't want you to know.

The Power of Ritual and Symbolism

To understand why the elite are so obsessed with rituals and symbols, we first need to delve into what these things actually do. In most cultures, rituals have been used for centuries as a way to connect with the divine, manifest desires, or bring about change. But rituals aren't just about calling on higher powers—they're about channeling human energy, focusing intention, and bending reality to the will of the practitioner.

Symbols, on the other hand, act as a kind of shorthand for complex ideas. They bypass the rational mind and speak directly to the subconscious, evoking emotions and reactions that aren't always immediately understood. This is why symbols are so powerful—and why they're everywhere, hidden in plain sight.

Now, imagine you have a small group of people who understand these concepts better than anyone else. They know which rituals unlock certain energies and which symbols can influence the minds of the masses. They use this knowledge not for the benefit of humanity, but for their own gain. This is the dark side of the occult practices of the elite.

Ancient Rituals and Modern Power

Let's take a trip back to ancient Babylon, Egypt, and Sumeria, where much of what we consider "modern" occult knowledge originates. In these civilizations, rituals and symbols were integral to governance and the maintenance of power. The priesthoods of these societies wielded immense power, often acting as the intermediaries between the gods and the people, and they used their knowledge to influence kings and shape the course of history.

Fast forward to today, and you'll see that many of these same practices have been adopted and adapted by modern elites. The use of sacred geometry in architecture, the alignment of buildings with celestial bodies, and the incorporation of ancient symbols in corporate logos all point to a deep understanding of the power of symbols and their ability to influence reality.

Take, for example, the Bohemian Grove, a private, male-only club in California where some of the world's most powerful men gather annually for two weeks. The Grove's attendees have included U.S. presidents, business magnates, and influential media figures. The centerpiece of the event is a ritual called the "Cremation of Care," which involves a mock human sacrifice in front of a giant owl statue, symbolizing the destruction of worldly concerns. While attendees and the press downplay this as harmless fun or mere theatrics, the symbolism and ritualistic elements suggest something much deeper—a connection to ancient rites that are meant to channel power and energy for those in the know.

The Occult Roots of Secret Societies

Many secret societies have their roots in occult practices and esoteric traditions. The Freemasons, for instance, are steeped in symbolism, with their rituals drawing heavily from the mystery schools of ancient Egypt and Greece. The Masonic rituals are designed to guide initiates through stages of enlightenment, revealing hidden knowledge and spiritual truths along the way. However, these rituals are also about control, binding members to secrecy, and creating a hierarchy where knowledge is power.

Similarly, the Rosicrucians, another secretive group, claim to possess esoteric knowledge passed down from ancient times. Their teachings blend elements of alchemy, Hermeticism, and Christian mysticism, with a strong emphasis on achieving spiritual enlightenment through ritual and study. But like the Freemasons, their practices also serve to create an inner circle of power, accessible only to those deemed worthy.

But it's not just about old European secret societies. Modern groups like the Ordo Templi Orientis (O.T.O.) and the Hermetic Order of the Golden Dawn have carried forward these traditions into the 20th and 21st centuries, blending Eastern and Western esoteric practices into a potent mix of rituals designed to unlock the power of the individual—and the group.

The question, then, is why these groups place such a heavy emphasis on ritual and secrecy. The answer lies in the power dynamics at play. By creating a system where knowledge is hidden behind layers of initiation and secrecy, these groups maintain control over their members and, by extension, over larger spheres of influence. Knowledge is hoarded, parceled out only to those who prove themselves worthy, and used to manipulate those who remain in the dark.

Modern-Day Occult Practices: From Hollywood to Politics

Occult symbolism isn't just hidden in secret societies; it's all around us, especially in popular culture and politics. Ever wonder why certain symbols keep popping up in movies, music videos, and even political campaigns? It's not a coincidence. The use of these symbols is a form of psychological manipulation, designed to condition the public and subtly influence their perceptions.

Take Hollywood, for example. The entertainment industry is rife with occult symbolism, from all-seeing eyes and pyramids to pentagrams and inverted crosses. These symbols are often dismissed as harmless artistic choices or Easter eggs for conspiracy theorists, but the truth is that they serve a deeper purpose. They're used to desensitize the public, to prepare them subconsciously for the agendas being pushed by those in power.

Even in politics, occult symbolism plays a role. Take a look at the architecture of government buildings in Washington, D.C., with their obelisks, domes, and Masonic layouts. Or consider the imagery used in political campaigns—stars, eagles, and other symbols that have deep esoteric meanings. These aren't just random choices; they're carefully crafted to convey messages to those in the know and to manipulate those who aren't.

Ritual Abuse and Darker Practices

We've talked about the more visible side of occult practices among the elite, but there's a much darker side that's rarely discussed—a side that involves ritual abuse and other horrifying practices. These are the whispers that make their way into conspiracy theories and underground forums, the stories that seem too shocking to be true but refuse to go away.

Ritual abuse is the systematic abuse of individuals, often children, in the context of a ritualistic framework. It's not just about physical abuse; it's about psychological manipulation, control, and the deliberate infliction of trauma to achieve specific goals, such as mind control or the creation of dissociative identities. These practices are alleged to be used by certain powerful groups to create programmable individuals who can be used as tools or pawns in their broader agendas.

There have been countless stories and testimonies over the years that suggest the existence of such practices among the elite. From the infamous Franklin scandal in the 1980s to more recent allegations involving high-profile figures, the idea that ritual abuse is used as a tool of control is both terrifying and plausible. While many of these stories are dismissed as conspiracy theories or urban legends, the sheer number of accounts and the consistency of the details suggest that there may be more to them than meets the eye.

Mind Control and Occult Practices

Mind control isn't just a concept for sci-fi movies; it's a documented reality with a long and disturbing history. Projects like MK-Ultra, run by the CIA, experimented with drugs, hypnosis, and other techniques to control and manipulate individuals. But what many don't realize is that these programs were often rooted in occult practices.

The use of ritual, trauma, and symbolism in mind control techniques draws directly from occult traditions. The idea is to break down the individual's sense of self, to shatter their reality and make them more susceptible to suggestion and control. It's a form of psychological alchemy, transforming a person's consciousness into something malleable and controllable.

This isn't just about government programs, either. There are countless accounts of individuals who claim to have been subjected to these kinds of practices by powerful groups, ranging from secret societies to religious cults. The goal is always the same: control, manipulation, and the exertion of power over another human being.

The Power of Secrecy: Why They Hide

Why all the secrecy? Why go to such lengths to hide these practices from the public? The answer is simple: power. The more people know about these practices, the less effective they become. The element of surprise, the ability to manipulate and control from behind the scenes, is lost when the game is exposed.

But there's another reason, too. If the public knew the full extent of what was happening behind closed doors, there would be an uproar. People would demand accountability, justice, and transparency. The carefully constructed narrative of benevolent leadership and democratic governance would crumble, and with it, the power of those who rely on secrecy and manipulation to maintain their control.

The truth is, they need us to be in the dark. They need us to be afraid, to be complacent, to accept the reality they've created for us. But once we start asking questions, once we start demanding the truth, their power begins to wane. Knowledge is power, and by uncovering these dark practices, we take the first step toward reclaiming our own.

Conclusion: The Path Ahead

So where do we go from here? Now that we've pulled back the curtain on the dark practices of the elite, it's up to us to decide what to do with this knowledge. This isn't just about exposing the truth; it's about taking action.

We need to start questioning everything. We need to demand transparency from our leaders and hold them accountable for their actions. We need to support independent media that isn't afraid to ask the hard questions and dig into the uncomfortable truths. And most importantly, we need to educate ourselves and others about the real nature of power and control in our world.

This is just the beginning of our journey. There are more secrets to uncover, more lies to expose, and more truths to be revealed. As we move forward, we must remember that knowledge is our greatest weapon in the fight against those who seek to control us. The more we know, the less power they have. So let's keep digging, keep questioning, and keep pushing forward.

The darkness is deep, but the light of truth is brighter. Are you ready to continue? Then let's dive deeper and see what else lies beneath the surface.

| 3 |

Chapter 3: Manipulation and Misdirection

If you've made it this far, you're already starting to see through the fog that's been purposefully laid over our eyes. We've looked at the power players pulling the strings from the shadows and the dark rituals they use to fuel their control. But now, it's time to talk about one of their most effective tools: manipulation and misdirection. This chapter is all about how the powerful control the masses, keeping us distracted, divided, and in the dark while they execute their plans behind closed doors.

From mass media to social engineering, we're going to break down the tactics used to keep you from seeing the bigger picture. These tactics aren't new—they've been honed over centuries, perfected through trial and error, and are now deployed with precision and subtlety that would make a magician jealous. The elite have mastered the art of misdirection, turning our attention wherever they want it, whenever they want it, all while hiding their true intentions in plain sight. It's time to expose the tricks and understand how they manipulate reality to maintain control.

The Media Machine: Manufacturing Consent

Let's start with one of the most powerful tools of manipulation: the media. If you think the media is just about delivering news and entertainment, think again. The media is a finely tuned machine designed to shape public opinion, create narratives, and control the flow of information. It's about manufacturing consent—convincing you to go along with things you might otherwise reject if you knew the full truth.

Edward Bernays, known as the father of public relations, once said, "The conscious and intelligent manipulation of the organized habits and opinions of the masses is an important element in democratic society." He wasn't wrong, and he wasn't kidding. The media, as it stands today, is an instrument of control, used to shape our beliefs, desires, and fears.

Think about how news is presented. It's not just about what's reported, but how it's reported. The language used, the images shown, the experts brought in to give their opinions—all of these elements are carefully curated to elicit a specific response. We're told who the heroes and villains are, what's important and what isn't, and what we should be focusing on at any given moment.

This isn't a conspiracy theory; it's media manipulation 101. By controlling what we see, hear, and read, the media shapes our perception of reality. It tells us what to care about and what to ignore, effectively keeping us distracted and misinformed. And who controls the media? A handful of corporations owned by a few powerful individuals, many of whom have deep ties to the very elite groups we've been talking about.

The Art of Distraction: Bread and Circuses

The concept of "bread and circuses" dates back to ancient Rome, where the government kept the populace content and distracted with free food and entertainment. Fast forward to today, and not much has changed. Modern distractions might look different—endless streams of social media, 24/7 news cycles, reality TV, and consumer culture—but the effect is the same: keep the masses entertained, and they won't ask questions.

The strategy of distraction is simple yet effective. When people are busy obsessing over the latest celebrity scandal, sports game, or Netflix series, they're not paying attention to what really matters. They're not questioning why their rights are being eroded, why the rich keep getting richer, or why the world seems to be constantly on the brink of disaster. They're too busy being entertained to notice the bigger picture.

But distraction goes beyond entertainment. It's also about creating crises and conflicts that keep us focused on each other instead of the real enemy. Divide and conquer has been a strategy used by rulers for centuries, and it's still in full effect today. Whether it's race, religion, political affiliation, or economic status, we're constantly being pitted against one another. The more divided we are, the easier we are to control. And while we're busy fighting amongst ourselves, the true Puppet Masters continue their work unimpeded.

False Flags and Psyops: Creating the Enemy

Let's talk about false flags and psychological operations (psyops). These are tactics used to manipulate the public into believing a certain narrative, often to justify actions that would otherwise be unacceptable. A false flag is an event that is staged or manipulated to appear as if it was carried out by someone else, usually an enemy or opposing force. The goal is to create fear, confusion, and a rallying cry for action.

History is filled with examples of false flags. The sinking of the USS Maine, which led to the Spanish-American War; the Reichstag fire, which allowed Hitler to consolidate power; and the Gulf of Tonkin incident, which escalated the Vietnam War—these are just a few cases where events were manipulated or staged to achieve a desired outcome.

Psyops are a bit different but equally insidious. These are operations designed to influence the emotions, motives, and behaviors of target audiences. They can take many forms, from propaganda campaigns to covert disinformation efforts. The goal is to create a specific psychological effect that supports a broader agenda.

Think about how fear has been used to manipulate the masses. Fear of terrorism, fear of economic collapse, fear of disease—these are powerful motivators that can be used to push through policies, restrict freedoms, and justify wars. When people are afraid, they're more likely to accept draconian measures, give up their rights, and look to authority figures for protection.

The Psychological Trap: Keeping You in Your Place

So, how do they keep us locked into this cycle of manipulation and distraction? The answer lies in psychology. Over the years, the elite have become masters at understanding how the human mind works, using that knowledge to keep us compliant and docile.

One of the most powerful psychological tools at their disposal is the concept of learned helplessness. This is a state where a person or group feels powerless to change their situation, even when they have the ability to do so. By creating a constant state of crisis, conflict, and fear, the Puppet Masters instill a sense of helplessness in the public. People start to believe that they have no control over their lives, that the problems are too big and complex to solve, and that the best they can do is to keep their heads down and try to get by.

But learned helplessness isn't the only trick up their sleeve. There's also cognitive dissonance, the discomfort we feel when holding two conflicting beliefs or attitudes. The elite use this to their advantage by bombarding us with contradictory information, confusing messages, and shifting narratives. This creates a sense of disorientation and anxiety, making people more susceptible to suggestion and control.

And then there's social proof—the idea that people are more likely to conform to the behavior of others in a group. This is why you see massive pushback against those who question the narrative. Dissenters are labeled as crazy, fringe, or dangerous, reinforcing the idea that it's safer to go along with the crowd than to think for oneself.

Digital Manipulation: The New Frontier

In the digital age, the tools of manipulation have become even more sophisticated. Social media platforms, search engines, and digital news outlets are all designed to keep you hooked, keep you scrolling, and keep you consuming content that reinforces certain narratives. Algorithms determine what you see and don't see, creating echo chambers where your existing beliefs are amplified, and opposing viewpoints are silenced or buried.

But it goes deeper than that. Digital surveillance and data collection mean that every click, every like, and every share is being tracked, analyzed, and used to build a profile of you—your likes, your dislikes, your fears, and your desires. This data is then used to serve you content, ads, and information that are specifically designed to manipulate you on a personal level.

And it's not just about selling you products. This data can be used to influence elections, sway public opinion, and shape the course of global events. We've already seen examples of this, from the Cambridge Analytica scandal to the spread of disinformation during elections. The digital world is the new battleground, and the weapons are algorithms and data.

Controlled Opposition: The Illusion of Choice

One of the most insidious tactics used by those in power is the concept of controlled opposition. This is where they create or co-opt movements, leaders, or organizations that appear to be fighting against the status quo, but are actually serving the interests of the elite. The goal is to give people the illusion of choice, to make them believe they have a voice and an avenue for change, while keeping them safely within the bounds of control.

Controlled opposition can take many forms. It could be a political party that claims to represent the people but is funded by the same corporate interests as their opponents. It could be a grassroots movement that starts with genuine intentions but is quickly infiltrated and steered by agents of the status quo. It could even be a charismatic leader who rallies the masses, only to betray them when it matters most.

The key to controlled opposition is to ensure that any resistance remains ineffective, disorganized, or easily discredited. By controlling both sides of the narrative, the Puppet Masters ensure that real change is impossible, and the system remains intact.

Breaking the Spell: How to See Through the Lies

So, how do we break free from this cycle of manipulation and control? The first step is awareness. You can't fight what you don't understand, and you can't see through the lies if you don't know they're there. By recognizing the tactics used to control us, we start to take back our power.

Next, we need to cultivate critical thinking and skepticism. Don't accept anything at face value. Question everything, especially the narratives being pushed by mainstream media and official sources. Look for the underlying motives, follow the money, and ask yourself who benefits from the information being presented.

We also need to take control of our own minds. This means breaking free from the cycle of distraction, turning off the noise, and focusing on what truly matters. It means being mindful of what we consume—both in terms of media and information—and being aware of how it affects our perceptions and beliefs.

Finally, we need to unite. The strategy of divide and conquer only works if we let it. By coming together, sharing information, and supporting one another, we can build a movement that's immune to manipulation and strong enough to challenge the status quo.

Conclusion: The Battle for Your Mind

The battle for control isn't fought with guns and tanks—it's fought in the mind. The Puppet Masters understand this, and they've honed their tactics to perfection. But now, the game is changing. People are waking up, asking questions, and demanding the truth. The more we understand their methods, the less power they have over us.

This chapter was about seeing through the smokescreen, recognizing the tactics of manipulation and control, and taking the first steps toward breaking free. But the journey doesn't end here. There's still more to uncover, more lies to expose, and more truth to reveal.

Are you ready to keep going? Then let's push forward and continue to dig deeper into the web of control. The truth is out there, waiting to be discovered. Let's find it together.

| 4 |

Chapter 4: The War on Human Potential

If you're still with me, then you're already starting to see the bigger picture—the puppet masters pulling strings from behind the scenes, the use of ritual and misdirection to manipulate the masses. But there's another layer to this game, one that's even more insidious and far-reaching: the war on human potential. This isn't just about controlling what you think or how you vote; it's about limiting who you are and what you can become.

The powers that be aren't satisfied with just keeping you distracted or misled; they want to keep you small, keep you from realizing your full potential. Why? Because an awakened, empowered individual is the biggest threat to their control. When people start to realize their true power, they begin to see through the lies, question the system, and take back control of their lives. This chapter is about uncovering the ways in which the elite suppress human potential, keeping us locked in a state of dependency, fear, and ignorance.

The Educational System: A Factory for Conformity

Let's start with one of the most fundamental tools of control: the education system. Now, you might think that education is about learning, expanding your mind, and developing critical thinking skills. And in an ideal world, it would be. But the reality is far from this ideal. The modern education system, especially in the West, was designed not to enlighten, but to condition.

The roots of our current system can be traced back to the Industrial Revolution, a time when the elite needed obedient workers who could read instructions, follow orders, and perform repetitive tasks without question. The education system was modeled after the factory, with its bells, rigid schedules, and emphasis on rote memorization. It was about producing a standardized product, not nurturing individual potential.

Think about it: from a young age, children are taught to sit still, obey authority, and regurgitate information. Creativity is stifled, curiosity is discouraged, and the focus is always on conformity. The system rewards those who can memorize and repeat, not those who think outside the box or challenge the status quo. And this is by design. An educated, critically thinking population is much harder to control than a herd of compliant sheep.

But it goes even deeper. Standardized testing, a cornerstone of modern education, isn't about measuring intelligence or potential. It's about enforcing a narrow worldview, one that values compliance over creativity, obedience over originality. The tests measure not what you know or how you think, but how well you can conform to the expected answers. It's a subtle form of mind control, conditioning young minds to think inside the box and discouraging them from venturing outside it.

The Pharmaceutical Industry: Chemical Control

Now, let's shift gears and talk about another major tool in the war on human potential: the pharmaceutical industry. We live in a world where there's a pill for every problem, a chemical solution for every ailment. But what if I told you that this industry, far from being about healing, is actually about control?

The pharmaceutical industry, with its billions of dollars in profits, is one of the most powerful entities on the planet. And it's not just about money; it's about control. By medicating the population, they're able to keep people docile, dependent, and numb. Drugs that are supposed to treat anxiety, depression, and ADHD often have side effects that dull the mind, suppress emotions, and reduce the capacity for critical thinking.

And then there's the war on consciousness—a deliberate effort to suppress substances that expand the mind, open new avenues of perception, and challenge the status quo. Psychedelics like LSD, psilocybin, and DMT, once hailed for their potential to treat mental illness and expand consciousness, were demonized and made illegal. Why? Because they represented a threat to the established order. They offered a glimpse of a reality beyond the material, a world where the mind was not just a byproduct of the brain, but a powerful tool capable of shaping reality itself.

The criminalization of these substances wasn't about protecting public health; it was about protecting the status quo. The elite fear an awakened population, a group of people who have experienced altered states of consciousness and realized that reality is not as rigid and controlled as they've been led to believe. So they suppress these substances, pushing instead their own drugs, ones that dull the senses and keep people firmly grounded in the reality they've constructed.

Technology: The Double-Edged Sword

Technology is another battleground in the war on human potential. On the one hand, it offers incredible opportunities for connection, learning, and empowerment. On the other, it's a tool of control, surveillance, and distraction. The internet, social media, smartphones—these are all double-edged swords, capable of both liberating and enslaving.

Let's talk about social media for a moment. What was supposed to be a platform for free expression has become a tool for mass manipulation. Algorithms determine what content you see, keeping you in a bubble of like-minded opinions and filtering out anything that might challenge your views. This creates echo chambers where critical thinking is stifled, and dissenting voices are drowned out by the noise.

And then there's the issue of surveillance. Every click, every like, every share is tracked and monitored, building a detailed profile of who you are, what you think, and how you can be manipulated. This data is then used to serve you targeted ads, influence your behavior, and shape your perceptions. It's not just about selling you products; it's about shaping your reality.

And don't even get me started on screen addiction. The constant barrage of notifications, updates, and alerts keeps you in a state of perpetual distraction, unable to focus on the bigger picture or engage in deep, meaningful thought. It's a digital leash, keeping you tethered to a device that's designed to control your attention and, by extension, your mind.

The Cult of Materialism: Chasing Shadows

Materialism is another tool used to keep you in line. We're taught from a young age that success is measured by what we own, that happiness comes from external possessions, and that the key to fulfillment lies in consumption. This is the cult of materialism, and it's a powerful form of control.

Think about it: if you're constantly chasing the next big thing, the latest gadget, the newest car, you're always looking outside yourself for validation and happiness. You become trapped in a cycle of desire and dissatisfaction, never realizing that true fulfillment comes from within. This keeps you locked into a system that's designed to exploit your desires and keep you running on a hamster wheel of consumption.

But it's not just about keeping you distracted; it's about keeping you compliant. People who are focused on material wealth are less likely to question the system, challenge authority, or seek deeper truths. They're too busy trying to keep up with the Joneses to notice that the game is rigged against them.

The Suppression of Spirituality: Disconnecting You from Your True Self

One of the most effective ways to suppress human potential is to disconnect people from their true selves, and this is where the suppression of spirituality comes into play. I'm not talking about organized religion, which often serves as another tool of control, but true spirituality—the understanding that we are more than just physical beings, that we have a connection to something greater than ourselves.

From the burning of witches in the Middle Ages to the modern-day dismissal of alternative spirituality as "woo-woo," there's been a concerted effort to suppress any form of spiritual practice that empowers the individual and challenges the established order. Meditation, energy work, psychic abilities—these are all dismissed, ridiculed, or outright banned in some cultures. Why? Because they represent a threat to the materialist worldview that keeps people in line.

When people realize their true nature as spiritual beings, they start to see through the illusions that have been cast over them. They begin to question the narrative, to challenge the system, and to seek out their own truths. This is why the elite fear spirituality—it represents a path to empowerment, one that leads away from their control and toward true freedom.

The Fear Factor: Keeping You in a Low Vibration

Fear is another powerful tool used to suppress human potential. When people are afraid, they're easy to control. They're more likely to accept authority, give up their rights, and go along with the status quo. This is why the media is filled with stories of crime, disaster, and conflict. It's why politicians use fear to push through policies and why corporations use fear to sell products.

But fear doesn't just control behavior; it also suppresses consciousness. When you're in a state of fear, your vibration is low. You're disconnected from your higher self, your intuition, and your inner wisdom. You're operating from a place of survival, not creation, and this keeps you from realizing your full potential.

The elite know this, and they use fear to keep you in line. They create crises, real or imagined, to keep you in a state of anxiety and uncertainty. They use fear to divide us, to keep us fighting amongst ourselves rather than uniting against a common enemy. And they use fear to keep us from looking within, from realizing that we are far more powerful than we've been led to believe.

Breaking Free: Reclaiming Your Power

So, how do we break free from this war on human potential? The first step is awareness—understanding the tactics used to keep you small, distracted, and disconnected. Once you see the game for what it is, you can start to take back your power.

Education is key, but not the kind you get in school. It's about educating yourself, seeking out knowledge that challenges the status quo, and developing critical thinking skills that allow you to see through the lies. It's about learning to think for yourself, to question everything, and to seek out your own truths.

Next, we need to reconnect with our true selves. This means exploring spirituality, meditation, and other practices that help us connect with our higher selves and realize our true potential. It means breaking free from the cult of materialism and realizing that true fulfillment comes from within, not from external possessions.

We also need to take control of our health and well-being. This means questioning the pharmaceutical industry, seeking out alternative therapies, and being mindful of what we put into our bodies and minds. It means taking back control of our own healing and rejecting the idea that we need a pill for every problem.

And finally, we need to overcome fear. This doesn't mean ignoring the challenges we face, but rather facing them with courage, confidence, and a sense of empowerment. It means recognizing that fear is a tool of control and refusing to let it dictate our lives.

Conclusion: Awakening the Giant Within

The war on human potential is real, but it's a war we can win. The tools of control are powerful, but they're not insurmountable. By awakening to our true potential, we can break free from the chains that bind us and reclaim our power.

This chapter was about exposing the tactics used to keep us small, dependent, and disconnected. But it's also about empowerment—about realizing that we are far more powerful than we've been led to believe. The journey to reclaim our potential is not an easy one, but it's a journey worth taking.

Are you ready to continue this journey? To awaken the giant within and realize your true potential? Then let's keep going. The path ahead is challenging, but the rewards are immense. Let's take the next step together and continue to uncover the truth.

| 5 |

Chapter 5: Lost History – The Secrets of Our Past

Alright, we've uncovered the puppet masters, exposed their dark rituals, dissected their methods of manipulation, and revealed their war on human potential. But if you think that's the whole story, you're wrong. This next chapter is going to shake you to your core because it's about what they don't want you to know about our past. History, as we know it, is a construct. It's a story written by the victors, a narrative shaped to fit a particular agenda. There are vast swathes of human history that have been hidden, erased, or outright fabricated to keep us in the dark about who we are, where we come from, and what we're truly capable of.

This chapter is a deep dive into the lost and hidden histories of our world, the secrets buried beneath layers of lies and misdirection. We're going to uncover ancient civilizations, suppressed knowledge, and the untold stories that could change everything we think we know about humanity and our place in the universe.

The Great Forgetting: How History Is Shaped

Before we dig into specific examples, let's talk about how history gets written—or rewritten. Imagine history as a vast tapestry, each thread representing a piece of the human experience. Now, imagine those in power pulling out threads they don't like and weaving in new ones to suit their narrative. This isn't just a metaphor; it's the reality of how history has been shaped for centuries.

Throughout time, conquerors, kings, and religious leaders have erased or altered history to maintain control and justify their rule. They've destroyed libraries, burned books, and silenced voices that dared to tell a different story. The Great Library of Alexandria, for example, was once the largest repository of knowledge in the ancient world. It's said to have housed texts on everything from science and philosophy to mysticism and magic. But after multiple fires and a campaign of destruction, much of this knowledge was lost forever—or so we're told.

But this rewriting of history isn't just ancient history; it's still happening today. School textbooks present a sanitized, simplified version of events, omitting the uncomfortable truths and alternative perspectives. Historians who challenge the mainstream narrative are often marginalized, their work discredited or ignored. The result is a collective amnesia, a great forgetting of who we are and where we came from.

Ancient Civilizations: The Suppressed Evidence

Let's talk about ancient civilizations—those mysterious, advanced societies that existed long before our own. The mainstream narrative tells us that human civilization began about 6,000 years ago with the Sumerians and then progressed in a straight line through Egypt, Greece, Rome, and into modern times. But what if that's not the whole story? What if there were advanced civilizations that existed tens of thousands of years ago, long before recorded history, that were wiped out and forgotten?

Take Göbekli Tepe, a site in modern-day Turkey that's been dated to around 12,000 years ago—7,000 years older than Stonehenge and the Great Pyramid of Giza. This site challenges everything we thought we knew about the timeline of human civilization. It's an intricate complex of stone pillars, many of which are covered in detailed carvings of animals and abstract symbols. But here's the kicker: it was intentionally buried by its builders, as if they wanted to preserve it for future generations or hide it from someone—or something.

Then there's the story of Atlantis, an advanced civilization that supposedly existed over 10,000 years ago and was lost to a cataclysmic event. Plato described Atlantis as a powerful and technologically advanced society that disappeared in a single day and night. For centuries, mainstream historians dismissed Atlantis as a myth, but new archaeological findings suggest that there may be some truth to the legend. Discoveries of submerged cities, advanced ancient technologies, and unexplained artifacts all point to the possibility that there was once a great civilization that was lost to history.

And what about the pyramids? The Great Pyramid of Giza is one of the most studied and yet least understood structures in the world. Mainstream archaeologists claim it was built as a tomb for the Pharaoh Khufu around 4,500 years ago, but there's no evidence to support this. No burial chamber, no inscriptions, no mummies—nothing. The pyramid's construction techniques are still a mystery, with blocks weighing several tons fitted together with such precision that a razor blade can't fit between them. Could this be the work of a civilization far older and more advanced than we're led to believe?

Hidden Knowledge: The Lost Teachings

So why hide this history? Why suppress evidence of advanced ancient civilizations and the knowledge they possessed? The answer lies in control. Knowledge is power, and those who control knowledge control the narrative, and by extension, control society. If the public were to discover that there were advanced civilizations before ours, it would shatter the narrative that our current society is the pinnacle of human achievement. It would force us to rethink everything we know about human potential, technology, and the progression of history.

Consider the ancient practice of alchemy, which is often dismissed as a pseudo-science or precursor to chemistry. But alchemy wasn't just about turning lead into gold; it was a complex spiritual and philosophical system that explored the transformation of the soul and the nature of reality itself. The alchemists believed that the material and spiritual worlds were connected, and that by understanding one, you could understand the other. This knowledge was suppressed by the Church, which saw it as a threat to its authority. The alchemists were persecuted, their texts burned, and their teachings driven underground.

Or look at the ancient knowledge of healing and medicine. Indigenous cultures around the world have long possessed sophisticated knowledge of plant medicine and healing practices. But when European colonizers arrived, this knowledge was often dismissed as primitive or superstitious, and the healers were persecuted or forced to convert to Christianity. This knowledge was suppressed, replaced by Western medicine, which focuses on treating symptoms rather than addressing the root causes of disease.

And then there's the knowledge of consciousness itself. Many ancient cultures believed that human consciousness had the potential to connect with higher dimensions, access universal knowledge, and even influence physical reality. Practices like meditation, astral projection, and energy work were developed to explore and expand consciousness. But these practices were suppressed or dismissed as unscientific, ridiculed by a society that values materialism over spirituality, and control over freedom.

The Mystery Schools: Gatekeepers of Hidden Truths

To truly understand the suppression of knowledge, we need to talk about the mystery schools. These were secret institutions in ancient Egypt, Greece, Rome, and other civilizations where knowledge was guarded and only shared with those deemed worthy. The teachings of the mystery schools covered everything from mathematics and astronomy to philosophy, medicine, and magic. They believed that this knowledge was sacred, too powerful for the uninitiated, and needed to be protected from misuse.

The initiates of these schools underwent rigorous training and initiation rites designed to test their commitment and ability to handle the knowledge they were about to receive. The most famous of these schools was the Eleusinian Mysteries in ancient Greece, where initiates were taught the secrets of life, death, and rebirth through a series of rituals that remain shrouded in secrecy to this day.

The mystery schools weren't just about preserving knowledge; they were also about control. By keeping this knowledge hidden, they maintained their influence over society. The initiates often went on to become priests, philosophers, and leaders, using their knowledge to guide and manipulate the masses. The teachings of the mystery schools have been passed down through the ages, often hidden in plain sight within secret societies, religious texts, and symbols.

Suppressed Technologies: What They Don't Want You to Know

There's another aspect to this hidden history that's equally important: the suppression of advanced technologies. Throughout history, there have been countless examples of inventions and discoveries that have been suppressed, buried, or outright stolen to protect the interests of the elite.

Take Nikola Tesla, for example. Tesla was a brilliant inventor who developed technologies that could have changed the world. He discovered a way to transmit electricity wirelessly, developed a method for harnessing free energy from the Earth, and even claimed to have developed a weapon that could end all wars. But much of his work was suppressed, his funding cut, and his inventions stolen or destroyed by those who saw him as a threat to the status quo.

Or consider the work of Wilhelm Reich, a psychoanalyst and scientist who discovered what he called "orgone energy," a universal life force that he believed could be harnessed for healing and weather control. Reich's work was ridiculed, his books burned, and he was eventually imprisoned by the U.S. government, dying in prison under mysterious circumstances.

And let's not forget about the countless patents for inventions that could have revolutionized energy, medicine, and technology, only to be bought up and suppressed by corporations and governments. Cold fusion, anti-gravity technology, and free energy devices—these aren't the stuff of science fiction, but real inventions that have been hidden from the public to protect the interests of those in power.

The Role of Religion: Controlling the Narrative

Religion has also played a significant role in shaping our understanding of history and suppressing alternative narratives. Throughout history, religious institutions have been powerful forces of control, using doctrine and dogma to shape the beliefs and behaviors of the masses. But they've also been gatekeepers of knowledge, deciding what truths are shared and what are hidden.

Consider the story of Jesus Christ. The version we're taught in Sunday school is just one interpretation of a much more complex and nuanced history. Early Christianity was a diverse and decentralized movement, with different sects and beliefs about who Jesus was and what his teachings meant. But when the Roman Emperor Constantine converted to Christianity in the 4th century, he convened the Council of Nicaea to establish a unified doctrine. Texts that didn't conform to this doctrine were labeled heretical, and many were destroyed or hidden away.

The same goes for other religious traditions. The Vedic texts of ancient India contain sophisticated knowledge of mathematics, astronomy, and spirituality, but much of this knowledge was suppressed by the British during their colonization of India. Indigenous religions and practices were often labeled as "pagan" or "savage" and were systematically eradicated or assimilated into dominant religious frameworks.

Why This Matters: The Power of Hidden History

So why does this matter? Why should we care about lost civilizations, suppressed knowledge, and hidden technologies? Because history shapes our identity, our beliefs, and our understanding of what's possible. When we don't know our true history, we don't know our true potential.

The suppression of history isn't just about controlling the past; it's about controlling the future. By keeping us ignorant of our true origins, the elite keep us in a state of dependency, fear, and complacency. They make us believe that we're the pinnacle of human achievement, that our current way of life is the best we can hope for, and that any alternative is either impossible or undesirable.

But when we uncover these hidden histories, we begin to see the cracks in the narrative. We start to realize that we're capable of so much more than we've been led to believe, that we have a rich heritage of knowledge, wisdom, and achievement that has been hidden from us. We begin to see through the lies, question the official story, and reclaim our true power.

Conclusion: Reclaiming Our Past, Reclaiming Our Power

The lost history of our world is a story of potential—potential that has been hidden, suppressed, and denied to us by those who seek to control us. But it's also a story of hope, a reminder that we are more than what we've been told, that our past is richer and more complex than we've been led to believe.

This chapter was about uncovering the hidden truths of our history, challenging the narrative that has been constructed for us, and reclaiming the knowledge that has been lost. It's about understanding that history is not a straight line but a tapestry, a web of interconnected stories, truths, and possibilities that have been deliberately hidden from us.

The journey to uncover our lost history is not an easy one, but it's a journey worth taking. It's a journey that requires us to question everything, to seek out the truth, and to challenge the official story. It's a journey that empowers us to reclaim our true potential and to create a future that is worthy of our past.

Are you ready to continue this journey? To dig deeper into the hidden truths of our world and to reclaim the knowledge that has been lost? Then let's keep going. The truth is out there, waiting to be discovered. Let's find it together.

| 6 |

Chapter 6: Taking Back Control – Breaking Free

So far, we've uncovered the dark secrets of those who pull the strings behind the scenes, revealed the rituals and symbols that bind their power, and exposed the ways they manipulate and control the masses. We've delved into the war on human potential and uncovered the hidden histories that they don't want us to know. But now it's time to turn the lens inward, to shift from understanding the game to breaking free from it. This chapter is about reclaiming your power and taking back control of your own life.

If there's one thing you need to know, it's this: the power structures we've been talking about only have as much control as we allow them to have. The greatest secret of all is that we are far more powerful than we've been led to believe. The systems of control rely on our ignorance, our compliance, and our belief in their narratives. Once we start questioning, once we start waking up, the entire house of cards begins to collapse.

This chapter will lay out a roadmap for breaking free from the systems of control. We'll explore practical strategies for reclaiming your mind, understanding your true self, and living a life that's true to your values and potential. It's time to step out of the shadows and into the light, to break the chains that have been holding you back and reclaim your sovereignty.

Step 1: Reclaim Your Mind

The first step in taking back control is to reclaim your mind. This might sound simple, but it's probably the hardest part of all. The truth is, we've all been conditioned to think in certain ways, to accept certain narratives, and to believe certain things about ourselves and the world. Breaking free from this conditioning requires conscious effort, critical thinking, and a willingness to question everything you've ever been taught.

Start by turning off the noise. The constant barrage of media, social media, and digital distractions keeps your mind in a state of perpetual reaction. Turn off the TV, delete the social media apps from your phone, and give yourself space to think, to reflect, and to reconnect with your inner voice.

Begin questioning the narratives you've been fed. Why do you believe what you believe? Who benefits from these beliefs? Look for the gaps in the stories, the contradictions, and the things that don't add up. Be willing to challenge your assumptions and explore alternative perspectives, even if they make you uncomfortable.

Practice mindfulness and meditation. These practices help you become more aware of your thoughts, allowing you to observe them without getting caught up in them. When you meditate, you create a space of awareness between you and your thoughts, giving you the power to choose which thoughts to engage with and which to let go.

Step 2: Reconnect with Your True Self

Once you've started reclaiming your mind, the next step is to reconnect with your true self. This is about getting in touch with who you really are, beyond the labels, the roles, and the identities that have been imposed on you by society. It's about understanding your true nature as a spiritual being, a creator, and a sovereign individual.

Spend time in nature. Nature has a way of grounding us, of helping us reconnect with our true essence. Take regular breaks from the concrete jungle and spend time in the natural world. Go for walks in the woods, sit by the ocean, or simply spend time in your garden. Allow yourself to feel the earth beneath your feet, the wind on your skin, and the sun on your face.

Engage in self-reflection and journaling. Ask yourself the big questions: Who am I? What do I want from life? What are my true values? What makes me happy? Use a journal to explore these questions and to reconnect with your inner self. Be honest with yourself, and don't be afraid to confront the uncomfortable truths that may arise.

Explore spirituality. This doesn't mean you have to follow a particular religion or belief system. It's about exploring your own spiritual path and discovering what resonates with you. This could involve practices like meditation, yoga, energy work, or simply spending time in quiet contemplation. The goal is to reconnect with your higher self and to understand your place in the universe.

Step 3: Break Free from Materialism

One of the most effective tools of control is materialism—the belief that our worth is determined by what we own, that happiness comes from external possessions, and that success is measured by wealth and status. Breaking free from materialism is about recognizing that true fulfillment comes from within, not from the accumulation of stuff.

Simplify your life. Start by decluttering your physical space. Get rid of the things you don't need, that don't bring you joy, or that don't serve a purpose in your life. This isn't just about cleaning out your closet; it's about letting go of the things that are holding you back, that are keeping you tethered to a lifestyle that isn't aligned with your true values.

Reevaluate your relationship with money. Money is a tool, not a goal. It's something that should serve you, not the other way around. Start by examining your spending habits. Are you spending money on things that truly bring you joy and fulfillment, or are you trying to fill a void? Shift your focus from accumulating wealth to creating experiences, building relationships, and pursuing your passions.

Practice gratitude. One of the best ways to break free from materialism is to cultivate a sense of gratitude for what you already have. Spend time each day reflecting on the things you're grateful for, whether it's your health, your relationships, or the simple pleasures of life. When you focus on what you have, rather than what you lack, you create a mindset of abundance that's resistant to the pull of materialism.

Step 4: Take Responsibility for Your Health

Your body is your temple, and taking care of it is one of the most powerful acts of sovereignty you can perform. The systems of control rely on keeping people sick, tired, and dependent on pharmaceuticals. Taking responsibility for your health is about reclaiming your power and recognizing that you have the ability to heal yourself.

Educate yourself about nutrition and natural healing. The mainstream medical system is heavily influenced by the pharmaceutical industry, which focuses on treating symptoms rather than addressing root causes. Take the time to learn about nutrition, herbal medicine, and other natural healing modalities. Understand the power of food as medicine and learn how to nourish your body with whole, nutrient-dense foods.

Detoxify your body and mind. Our bodies are constantly bombarded with toxins—from the food we eat to the air we breathe and the products we use. Consider doing a detox to help your body eliminate these toxins and reset your system. But detoxification isn't just physical; it's also mental and emotional. Take time to release negative emotions, limiting beliefs, and toxic thought patterns that are holding you back.

Move your body. Exercise isn't just about staying in shape; it's about connecting with your body, releasing stress, and increasing your vitality. Find a form of movement that you enjoy, whether it's dancing, hiking, yoga, or martial arts, and make it a regular part of your routine. When you move your body, you release stagnant energy, increase your endorphins, and reconnect with your physical self.

Step 5: Build Your Community

One of the most effective ways to break free from the system is to build a community of like-minded individuals who share your values, goals, and vision for the future. We're stronger together, and by supporting each other, we can create a network of resilience and empowerment that's immune to manipulation and control.

Find your tribe. Look for groups, organizations, and communities that align with your values and beliefs. This could be a local group focused on sustainability, a spiritual community, or an online forum where people discuss alternative perspectives. Surround yourself with people who challenge you, inspire you, and support you on your journey.

Practice mutual aid. Mutual aid is about helping each other out, sharing resources, and building resilience together. This could involve starting a community garden, organizing a skill-sharing workshop, or simply being there for a friend in need. By practicing mutual aid, you strengthen your community and build a network of support that's independent of the system.

Create a culture of empowerment. Our culture often glorifies negativity, division, and fear. But you have the power to create a different kind of culture—one that values empowerment, unity, and love. Be mindful of the energy you bring to your interactions, and strive to create spaces where people feel safe, supported, and uplifted. This isn't just about changing your own mindset; it's about changing the culture around you.

Step 6: Embrace Your Sovereignty

At the end of the day, breaking free from the system is about embracing your sovereignty—your inherent right to govern yourself, make your own decisions, and live life on your own terms. This is about recognizing that you are the creator of your reality, that you have the power to shape your life, and that you are not beholden to any authority outside yourself.

Set clear boundaries. Sovereignty starts with setting boundaries—with yourself, with others, and with society. This means knowing what you will and won't accept in your life, standing up for your rights, and refusing to compromise your values. Boundaries aren't about building walls; they're about creating a space where you can thrive.

Live with intention. Sovereignty also means living with intention, being deliberate about your choices, and aligning your actions with your values and goals. Take the time to reflect on what matters most to you and make decisions that are in alignment with your highest good. This could involve setting goals, creating a vision board, or simply taking a few moments each day to remind yourself of your intentions.

Claim your power. Finally, sovereignty is about claiming your power—your power to create, to heal, to love, and to live authentically. This means letting go of the victim mindset and embracing the fact that you are the author of your own story. It means recognizing that, while you can't control everything that happens in your life, you can control how you respond to it.

Conclusion: The Journey of Empowerment

Breaking free from the system isn't a one-time event; it's a journey—a journey of self-discovery, empowerment, and transformation. It's about reclaiming your mind, your body, your spirit, and your community. It's about stepping into your power and living a life that's true to who you are.

This chapter was about laying out the roadmap for taking back control, for breaking free from the chains that have been holding you back and reclaiming your sovereignty. It's a journey that requires courage, commitment, and perseverance, but it's a journey worth taking.

Are you ready to take the next step? To embrace your sovereignty, reclaim your power, and live a life that's true to your highest potential? Then let's keep going. The journey is just beginning, and there's so much more to discover. Let's take the next step together and continue to uncover the truth.

CONCLUSION: NOW YOU KNOW

We've reached the end of this journey, but in many ways, it's just the beginning. You've taken the time to dive deep into the murky waters of control, manipulation, and hidden truths. You've uncovered the Puppet Masters pulling the strings, the dark rituals that bind their power, and the layers of deceit that keep the masses in check. You've peeled back the veil on the war against human potential, revealing how our true capabilities have been systematically suppressed. You've explored the secrets of our lost history, learning that what we've been taught is just the tip of a vast iceberg of hidden knowledge.

But now, it's time to step back and see the bigger picture. The systems of control we've been talking about aren't invincible. They're fragile, built on a foundation of lies, secrecy, and manipulation. And now that you know the truth, they've lost some of their power. The knowledge you've gained isn't just information; it's a tool, a weapon you can use to reclaim your life and challenge the narratives that have been forced upon you.

What We've Uncovered

Throughout this book, we've exposed the many ways in which the powerful maintain their grip on the world. We've talked about secret societies, dark rituals, and the manipulation of public perception through media and misinformation. We've looked at how they suppress human potential, keeping us in a constant state of distraction, fear, and compliance. And we've revealed the hidden histories that show us a world far different from what we've been led to believe.

These revelations are more than just interesting facts; they're the key to understanding the true nature of power and control. They show us that the world isn't what it seems, that much of what we've been told is a carefully constructed illusion designed to keep us compliant and unaware.

The Power of Knowledge

Knowledge is power—real power. The more you know, the less control they have over you. This isn't about memorizing facts or reciting conspiracy theories; it's about understanding the forces that shape our world and recognizing the patterns of manipulation and control. It's about seeing through the lies, questioning the narratives, and refusing to be a pawn in someone else's game.

With knowledge comes awareness, and with awareness comes the ability to make different choices. Choices that aren't based on fear, manipulation, or falsehoods, but on truth, authenticity, and empowerment. This is the real power that the elite fear—the power of an informed, awakened individual who sees through their game and refuses to play by their rules.

Your Role in the New Narrative

Now that you've uncovered these truths, you have a choice to make. You can return to the comfort of ignorance, pretending you never learned what you now know. Or you can step into your role as a truth-seeker, a warrior for awareness, and a creator of a new narrative—one that's built on transparency, empowerment, and freedom.

This doesn't mean you have to become a full-time activist or conspiracy theorist. It means living your life with intention, questioning everything, and making choices that align with your values and your highest potential. It means refusing to be a passive participant in the stories others are telling about your life and instead becoming the author of your own story.

The Journey Ahead

The journey to reclaiming your power and breaking free from the systems of control is not an easy one. It requires courage, resilience, and a willingness to confront uncomfortable truths. But it's a journey worth taking, not just for yourself, but for the future of humanity.

Imagine a world where people are no longer controlled by fear, manipulation, or deception. A world where individuals are free to explore their true potential, to connect with their true selves, and to create a reality that reflects their highest ideals. This isn't some utopian fantasy; it's a real possibility, one that begins with awareness, knowledge, and action.

Final Thoughts

You are not alone in this journey. There are others, like you, who are waking up, asking questions, and seeking the truth. Together, we can create a movement that challenges the status quo, that pushes back against the systems of control, and that builds a future based on empowerment, freedom, and truth.

Remember, the most powerful weapon you have is your mind. Use it wisely. Question everything. Seek out knowledge. Trust your intuition. And most importantly, never stop searching for the truth.

The journey of awakening is not a destination but a continuous process of learning, growing, and evolving. You've taken the first step by opening your mind to the possibility that there's more to the world than what you've been told. Now, it's time to take the next step, and the next, and the next.

The truth is out there, waiting to be discovered. It's up to you to find it.

Are you ready? The world is waiting. The future is yours to create.

Now you know.

Demetri Welsh is a relentless seeker of truth, known for his raw and unfiltered approach to uncovering the hidden layers of reality. A former psychic reader, energy worker, and a successful musician, Demetri has spent decades challenging the status quo, delving into the metaphysical, and exposing the secrets that lie just beneath the surface. His experiences, from a tumultuous childhood to navigating the depths of spiritual and personal discovery, have forged a unique perspective that he brings to his writing.

As a published author and the voice behind thought-provoking blogs, Demetri dares to explore the dark and controversial topics that others shy away from. Through his work, he encourages readers to question everything, to embrace the unknown, and to reclaim their own power in a world designed to keep them in the dark. Demetri continues to share his insights and revelations through his writing, music, and his commitment to pushing the boundaries of what is known and what is hidden.

REFERENCES

The following sources have been referenced and consulted to provide the information and perspectives presented in this book. These references range from historical texts and academic studies to personal accounts, investigative journalism, and alternative research. They offer a diverse range of insights and are meant to encourage further exploration and critical thinking.

1. **Bernays, Edward L.** *Propaganda*. New York: Horace Liveright, 1928.

    ◦ A foundational text on the manipulation of public opinion, written by the father of public relations, this book provides insight into how media and propaganda shape societal beliefs and behaviors.

2. **Chomsky, Noam, and Edward S. Herman.** *Manufacturing Consent: The Political Economy of the Mass Media*. New York: Pantheon Books, 1988.

    ◦ This book explores the influence of corporate interests on media content and how this control shapes public perception and maintains the status quo.

3. **Childress, David H.** *Technology of the Gods: The Incredible Sciences of the Ancients*. Kempton, IL: Adventures Unlimited Press, 2000.

    ◦ An exploration of ancient technologies and civilizations, arguing that advanced knowledge existed long before modern recorded history suggests.

4. **Icke, David.** *The Biggest Secret: The Book That Will Change the World*. Scottsdale, AZ: Bridge of Love, 1999.

- A controversial book that delves into conspiracy theories, secret societies, and the hidden forces that Icke argues control global events.

5. **Quigley, Carroll.** *Tragedy and Hope: A History of the World in Our Time.* New York: Macmillan, 1966.

  - A historical study that examines the economic and political networks that Quigley argues have influenced world events from behind the scenes.

6. **Sitchin, Zecharia.** *The 12th Planet (Earth Chronicles, No. 1).* New York: Harper, 1976.

  - Sitchin's work on ancient astronaut theories and his interpretation of Sumerian texts suggests advanced extraterrestrial influence on early human civilizations.

7. **Tesla, Nikola.** *My Inventions: The Autobiography of Nikola Tesla.* Hart Brothers, 1983.

  - Tesla's autobiography provides insights into his life, inventions, and the challenges he faced from powerful interests that opposed his technological advancements.

8. **Weishaupt, Adam.** *Original Writings of the Illuminati.* Translated and Edited by John Robison. Charleston: Forgotten Books, 2018.

  - The original writings and ideas of the founder of the Illuminati, providing context and understanding of the goals and methods of this secret society.

9. **Plato.** *Timaeus and Critias.* Translated by Benjamin Jowett. Oxford: Oxford University Press, 1871.

  - These dialogues by Plato introduce the story of Atlantis, offering a glimpse into ancient philosophical ideas about civilization, cataclysm, and memory.

10.   **West, John Anthony, and Robert M. Schoch.** *The Sphinx Mystery: The Forgotten Origins of the Sanctuary of Anubis.* Rochester, VT: Inner Traditions, 2009.

   ◦ A discussion on the possible prehistoric origins of the Sphinx and implications for rethinking ancient Egyptian civilization's timeline.

11.   **Puharich, Andrija.** *The Sacred Mushroom: Key to the Door of Eternity.* New York: Doubleday, 1959.

   ◦ A study of the role of psychedelics in ancient spiritual practices and their potential to expand human consciousness.

12.   **McKenna, Terence.** *Food of the Gods: The Search for the Original Tree of Knowledge – A Radical History of Plants, Drugs, and Human Evolution.* New York: Bantam Books, 1992.

   ◦ An exploration of the impact of psychoactive plants on human culture and evolution, arguing that they played a significant role in the development of consciousness.

13.   **Hancock, Graham.** *Fingerprints of the Gods: The Evidence of Earth's Lost Civilization.* New York: Crown, 1995.

   ◦ Hancock's investigation into ancient myths, structures, and maps suggests the existence of an advanced global civilization that predates recorded history.

14.   **Mitchell, Edgar.** *The Way of the Explorer: An Apollo Astronaut's Journey Through the Material and Mystical Worlds.* New York: G. P. Putnam's Sons, 1996.

   ◦ Written by an astronaut, this book explores consciousness and the connection between quantum physics, spirituality, and the search for extraterrestrial life.

15.   **Robison, John.** *Proofs of a Conspiracy Against All the Religions and Governments of Europe.* Charleston: Forgotten Books, 2018.

- An early critique of secret societies, particularly the Illuminati, and their potential influence on political movements in Europe.

Additional Resources:

- **Articles, Documentaries, and Lectures**: There are numerous online resources, including articles, documentaries, and lectures that further explore the themes presented in this book. Websites like Gaia, TED Talks, and various independent researchers' platforms provide additional perspectives and evidence.
- **Academic Journals and Papers**: For a deeper dive into specific topics like ancient civilizations, mind control, and media manipulation, academic journals provide peer-reviewed studies and research that challenge mainstream narratives.
- **Historical Archives and Primary Sources**: When possible, go to the source. Many of the original writings, documents, and artifacts that inform alternative historical theories can be found in historical archives, museums, and digital repositories.

This list is by no means exhaustive but serves as a starting point for those interested in exploring further. Remember, the journey to truth is never-ending, and it requires a curious mind, a critical eye, and a fearless heart. Keep questioning, keep searching, and keep uncovering the hidden realities of our world.

www.ingramcontent.com/pod-product-compliance
Lightning Source LLC
Chambersburg PA
CBHW031225160726
47992CB00006B/2903